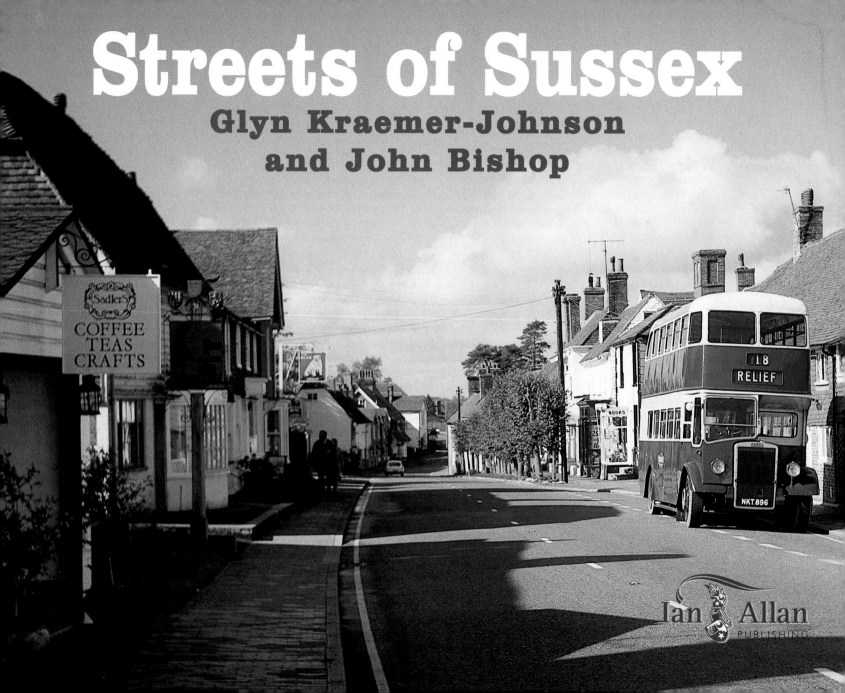

Streets of Sussex

Glyn Kraemer-Johnson
and John Bishop

Ian Allan PUBLISHING

Introduction

Everyone knows the song 'Sussex by the Sea', but there's an awful lot of the county that isn't. By the sea, that is. True, it has its seaside resorts, like the vibrant city of Brighton & Hove, now catering for a much younger clientele than it did in the late 'Forties and 'Fifties. Back then, on summer weekends, hundreds of coaches would arrive at Madeira Drive to disgorge their loads of day-trippers, mainly from London and the Home Counties. It is now possibly even more deserving of the epithet 'London-by-the-Sea' than it was when the phrase was first coined.

Along the coast are the resorts of Eastbourne and Worthing — a little more sedate, perhaps, but still offering a great deal for the tourist, and Eastbourne, at least, is still a popular base for coach touring holidays, one of the largest coach-tour operators even having its own hotel in the town. At the eastern end of the county is Hastings, falling somewhere between the two.

Almost on the Kent boundary is the quaint harbour town of Rye, whilst further west are the more commercial ports of Newhaven and Shoreham, the former being the departure point for ferries to Dieppe; its Harbour station once played host to a regular service of locomotive-hauled boat trains, but nowadays one is unlikely to see anything more exciting than an electric multiple-unit.

Inland, though not too far from the sea, are the County towns. The administrative centre for East Sussex is the historic town of Lewes, with its castle dating back almost to 1066, its narrow streets and plethora of antique shops. That for West Sussex is Chichester, the spire of whose fine Cathedral has dominated the skyline for miles around, also since not long after 1066, and whose Market Cross is just as much a landmark in the city itself. Arundel is possibly 'the Lewes of the west', with its magnificent castle (still occupied by the Duke of Norfolk), the River Arun running through the centre of the town and, once again, a multitude of antique shops.

The other inland towns, like Horsham, Haywards Heath and Uckfield, are pretty much as you might find anywhere, with their chain stores, industrial estates and rapidly spreading housing developments. An exception is Crawley, to the north of the county; this was expanded in the 'Fifties as a New Town to take London's overspill and has continued to expand both in size and importance, mainly due to its proximity to Gatwick Airport. Then there are the villages, some of which, like Alfriston and Mayfield, have become tourist attractions in their own right, whilst others, like Burwash and Ditchling, remain pretty much undisturbed. And between these towns and villages is the glorious Sussex countryside — the kind of countryside that makes the county's inhabitants wonder why they bother to go on holiday when there is such beauty on their doorstep.

The West Sussex coastal strip is pretty flat and uninteresting, but as it rises up towards Goodwood, Storrington and Midhurst the scenery becomes quite stunning, and there are some spectacular views across the Downs towards the coast. East of Brighton the coastal plain rises to form the white chalk cliffs which a little further east will become the Seven Sisters and culminate in the dramatic Beachy Head.

Stand on the Downs at Ditchling Beacon or Devil's Dyke and look down at the patchwork spread out below, travel through the leafy lanes and sleepy hamlets or drive along the road from Heathfield towards Kent — the spine of the Weald — and enjoy the panorama laid out before you and you will realise how much of the county remains unspoiled. There are no motorways as such,

---

Front cover: Traditionally Eastbourne was served by buses of both Southdown and Eastbourne Corporation. Looking smart in the mainly cream livery adopted from 1969, the latter's 57 (HJK 157), one of five East Lancs-bodied AEC Regent Vs delivered in 1961, is pursued along the town's Seaside thoroughfare by a newer example of this handsome combination, 65 (JJK 265). Of interest is that for many years the first digit of the registration of an Eastbourne bus matched the last digit of the year of its delivery; thus 65 was new in 1962. Nowadays the Woolworth's store, formerly the Regal Cinema, is itself long gone, although the building survives. *John Bishop*

Previous page: Located deep in East Sussex, the village of Burwash is famous for Batemans, one-time home of Rudyard Kipling. However, the High Street is the setting for this posed September 1976 view of preserved former Maidstone & District all-Leyland Titan PD2/12 DH400 (NKT 896), which at the time was owned by the photographer. The blinds, set to route 18, recall the route from Brighton to Hawkhurst, Kent, operated jointly with Southdown. *Dave Brown*

First published 2005

ISBN (10) 0 7110 3135 5
ISBN (13) 978 0 7110 3135 7

© Ian Allan Publishing Ltd 2005

Published by Ian Allan Publishing

an imprint of Ian Allan Publishing Ltd, Hersham, Surrey KT12 4RG
Printed in England by Ian Allan Printing Ltd, Hersham, Surrey KT12 4RG

Code: 0511/B1

Visit the Ian Allan Publishing website at www.ianallanpublishing.com

no huge industrial conurbations, but a remarkable amount of unblemished countryside.

Time was when all these villages and hamlets were served by bus. The apple-green-and-cream buses of Southdown Motor Services operated a comprehensive network of services throughout the county, carrying passengers to work, children to school, holidaymakers for an afternoon trip into the countryside, and even parcels, but they were not alone. In the east many of the services were operated jointly with the dark-green-and-cream buses of Maidstone & District. In the west Southdown met with the similarly liveried vehicles of Aldershot & District and to the north the Country Area buses of the mighty London Transport. Then there were the municipal operators. Eastbourne had a refreshing blue and primrose colour scheme whilst Brighton shared the red and cream of its bedfellow, the nationalised Brighton, Hove & District Omnibus Co. BH&D was the only Tilling-group company to operate trolleybuses, under a joint operating agreement with Brighton Corporation. This form of traction was also to be found in Hastings, where the trolleybuses of Hastings Tramways became a subsidiary of Maidstone & District and adopted the dark green and cream of the parent company.

Such was the scene until 1969, when the major operators became part of the National Bus Company and lost their individual liveries and identities. In 1986 came deregulation and, shortly afterwards, privatisation, since when there have been constant changes, with operators coming and going and services passing from one company to another with almost bewildering frequency.

The authors spent their formative years drinking in the delights of Southdown and Brighton, Hove & District in their original incarnations, and to us the 'Fifties and 'Sixties were very much the heyday of the Sussex bus. However, we realise that no-one under the age of 35 will recall seeing buses of this era in service, so we have stretched the boundaries a little to include some photographs from the NBC era and, indeed, a little later.

The photographs in this book are intended to illustrate the bus in Sussex, but beyond that we aim to depict the environment in which they worked, the street furniture, the buildings and the countryside — all those fragments, many half-forgotten, which go to make up 'dear old Sussex by the Sea'.

Finally, we would like to extend our thanks to all those who have contributed photographs for publication in this book and in particular to Patrick Jeffery of British Bookshops/Sussex Stationers, for the original idea.

Glyn Kraemer-Johnson
Hailsham, East Sussex
July 2005

Introduction by Glyn Kraemer-Johnson
Photographs selected and captioned by John Bishop

Above: An apparently timeless view of the north gateway to Brighton's famous Royal Pavilion — until the picture is studied in detail. Taken on a bright summer's day in the late 1930s, this early example of colour photography has the added bonus of a Class F Brighton Corporation tram, built at the Corporation's Lewes Road depot. Replaced by the trolleybus and motor bus, Brighton's trams would disappear in 1939, just before the outbreak of World War 2. The Tamplin's advertisement recalls another Sussex institution which has since passed into history, the brewery having closed in the 1960s.
D. Macdonald collection

Left: The picturesque East Sussex town of Rye was traditionally served by East Kent, which company's AEC Reliance/Weymann KFN 236, dating from 1955, is seen in Station Approach in May 1973. Under forthcoming reorganisation services in this area would pass to Maidstone & District, and the familiar red-and-cream buses would give way to NBC leaf green. As for the railway, following a battle for survival the line is an integral part of the transport system today, providing a link to the Eurostar Channel Tunnel terminal at Ashford, Kent. *John Bishop*

Below left: Hastings is notorious for its hilly terrain, as apparent from this view of Maidstone & District AEC Reliance/Harrington S196 (196 XKE). The bus was unusual in being built to 7ft 6in width and thus ideally suited to the narrow roads of both the town and surrounding villages; here it is making the long descent to the town centre on its way back from picturesque Fairlight, which name is believed to derive from 'Pharo's Light' (lighthouse). In the background is a contemporary BMC lorry with 'threepenny-bit' cab, so called because of its angular design. *Malcolm Keeping*

Right: A Willowbrook-bodied AEC Reliance delivered in 1962 after exhibition at that year's Commercial Motor Show, Maidstone & District S1 (984 TKO) prepares to climb Mount Pleasant Road, Hastings, *en route* to Ore on 5 August 1963. Four years previously the lamp standard (left) would have supported the wires for the trolleybuses which ran over this route. In the background is the Queens Road Bridge, which carries the railway line from Hastings to Ore, Rye and Ashford; note the semaphore signals still in use at this time. *Dave Warren*

Left: The year 2005 sees the 100th anniversary of Hastings Tramways, so it is perhaps fitting to illustrate a stretch of Hastings seafront served originally by trams as well as subsequently by trolleybuses and finally motor buses. Depicted is OT5 (FKO 229), a 1939 Leyland Titan TD5 with purpose-built open-top bodywork by Weymann, which, on account of its restricted seasonal use, would survive until 1965. This part of the seafront at Hastings remains instantly recognisable today.
Malcolm Keeping

Right: No book featuring Hastings would be complete without a view of the famous Norman castle overlooking the English Channel; an earthwork motte-and-bailey fortress, it was established by William the Conqueror. On the seafront on a seemingly cold and sunny day in the early 1970s we see three stages of Maidstone & District livery. On the left, heading away from the camera, is a Willowbrook-bodied Leyland Panther in traditional dark green but with NBC-style fleetname, while in the foreground, heading for Kent's County Town of Maidstone, is 2801 (OKO 801G), a 1968 Willowbrook-bodied Leyland Leopard still in full M&D dual-purpose livery, followed by a Weymann-bodied AEC Reliance bus newly painted in NBC leaf green. *Dave Brown*

Right: A feature of many towns is the annual carnival, and Hastings is no exception, as is apparent from this view of Maidstone & District Beadle-bodied AEC Regal 4003 (HKL 836) in the late 1970s. New in 1946 as a coach, this was one of three such vehicles converted to open-top in 1958. Happily the original cream livery, complete with traditional scroll fleetname, was retained in NBC days. *Dave Brown*

Left: When this photograph was taken in the early 1960s the photographer probably cursed that a car should have come into view at exactly the same time as his intended subject, but 40 years on it makes for a happy combination of the famous BMC Mini and the equally famous (in bus circles, anyway!) rear-engined Leyland Atlantean, both made in Great Britain. Dating from 1959, the latter, Weymann-bodied DL53 (53 DKT), was noteworthy not only in being of a type new to Maidstone & District but also by virtue of its lowbridge layout. The location is the Bull Inn, Bexhill Road, St Leonards-on-Sea, formerly a trolleybus terminus; note that the traction poles are still *in situ*, while in the background is evidence of the turning circle. Minus the trolley pole, the scene remains much the same today. *Malcolm Keeping*

Above: Bexhill-on-Sea has a strong Victorian/Edwardian feel by virtue of the number of buildings dating from the dawn of the 20th century. This scene, recorded on the town's seafront in March 1982, features a mixture of Edwardian, art-deco and postwar architecture. The bus, a Leyland National new in 1973 to Plymouth Corporation, is in service with Bexhill Town Bus Services, which independent operator was formed in 1980 following the withdrawal of local services hitherto provided by Maidstone & District. Note the concrete bus shelter, of a type once seen on many a highway but which has now given way to plastic/glass advertising shelters. *John Bishop*

Left: A study in perfect coach design, in the truly immaculate condition expected of Southdown Motor Services. Shortly after delivery in 1965 Leyland Leopard/ Harrington Grenadier 1755 (BUF 155C) takes a break at Pevensey Castle, in East Sussex. The building behind is no more, but otherwise the area is still recognisable today. Car 1755 was one of Southdown's last batch of Harrington-bodied coaches, which were built locally in Hove; regrettably Thos Harrington Ltd ceased production in the late 1960s, and its Sackville Works, which building survived until recently, has now given way to a retail park. *Howard Butler*

Above right: For those with long memories it is hard to believe there was ever a tramway in Eastbourne, yet until 1969 the 2ft-gauge Eastbourne Electric Tramway operated between Royal Parade/ Prince's Park and The Crumbles, car No 2 being seen leaving Prince's Park when almost new, on 2 August 1964. Today the system operates from Seaton in Devon and is hugely popular with tourists from all over the world. This car is still in service at Seaton, albeit re-gauged. *Dave Warren*

Right: Another view of Eastbourne Electric Tramway car No 2 in 1964, this time sparkling in the summer sun at The Crumbles. The Morris 8 Series E car parked by the terminus would today be a dream exhibit on the rally field. In recent times the area has been redeveloped as an extensive marina and housing complex, the only recognisable feature being the Martello Tower (visible here in the far distance), one of 74 built in the early 19th century to protect the South Coast from the threat of Napoleonic invasion. *Howard Butler*

Left: With the end of World War 2 and the gradual return to peacetime conditions came a greater emphasis on leisure time. One by-product of this trend was tourism, prompting operators to introduce open-top buses on scenic routes. Eastbourne Corporation was no exception, using ageing Leyland Titan PD1s with East Lancs bodywork, typified by 14 (JK 9112). This view, recorded on the seafront during the summer of 1968, shows it on route 6 to the Foot of Beachy Head; for many years only Southdown buses were permitted to climb to the top of this famous landmark. This scene, with the pier in the background, is little changed little today, even down to the ornate lamp standards. *Dave Brown*

Above right: Traditional Eastbourne Corporation fleet livery was an attractive application of blue and primrose, finished with a white roof. Bruce-bodied AEC Regent III 48 (AHC 448) is seen at 'The Archery'; situated near the Corporation's depot in Churchdale Road, this was where buses would lay over and change crews. A typical Eastbourne practice was the application of advertisements painted directly over the base colour of the bus, as seen here on the front and offside. Note also the large and informative bus-stop flag, leaving passengers in no doubt as to the destinations served. *Howard Butler*

Right: Some of the most attractive buses supplied to Eastbourne Corporation were the East Lancs-bodied AEC Regent Vs, represented by 67 (KHC 367) of 1963. This scene was recorded during the spring of 1973, when 67 was due a repaint into the cream livery already carried by the Leyland Panther behind. This area, known as Hampden Park, has since been built upon, and this view across the field has now been lost. *John Bishop*

Left: Photographed in 1975, Eastbourne 69 (KHC 369), an AEC Regent V with East Lancs bodywork, pauses outside Eastbourne railway station on the confusing interworked routes 1 and 4, bound for the bus stands at Terminus Road (behind the photographer). New to Eastbourne Corporation, the bus now has the 'EBC' logo, reflecting recent changes in local government; the local authority was now known as Eastbourne Borough Council, the town having lost its 'County Borough' status. Although 30 years have passed since this photograph was taken the scene remains just the same. No 69, meanwhile, was sold in 1980 for preservation but is still a regular visitor to its former home town. *Dave Brown*

Above right: Eastbourne 57 (HJK 157), an East Lancs-bodied AEC Regent V dating from 1961, threads its way along Terminus Road on route 4 to Langney, situated at the eastern end of town. The construction work on the right is for the Arndale shopping centre. Note the buildings on the right, often overlooked by visitors who are more intent on shopping than admiring the architecture. *Dave Brown*

Right: In 1973, when this view was recorded, Eastbourne Corporation still had a few elderly AEC Regent Vs from 1956 relegated to school and relief work. Devoid of advertisements, 53 (DHC 653) stands in Cornfield Road, whilst behind is the area where now stands the Arndale Centre, entailing the closure of Junction Road. *John Bishop*

Left: By 1980 the National Bus Company was a fact of life, but somehow Southdown still managed to give that little extra for its passengers. We still had bus stations instead of on-street stops, as here in Pevensey Road, Eastbourne. With Park Royal-bodied Leyland Atlantean 702 (PUF 132M) ready to depart for Brighton and dual-purpose Northern Counties-bodied Leyland Leopard 465 (PUF 165H) in the background, the signage above defiantly informs passengers that this is the 'SOUTHDOWN OMNIBUS STATION'. Needless to say, the bus station is long gone, and the site is now occupied in part by a night-time drinking establishment. *Dave Brown*

Above: The historic vulnerability of the South Coast to invasion is recalled by this mine on display to the public at Beachy Head, near Eastbourne, East Sussex. Judging by the German graffiti this view of Northern Counties-bodied Leyland PD3/4 410 (410 DCD) in full NBC leaf green was recorded in or soon after July 1978. By this time the vehicle was already 14 years old but nevertheless performed well up the steep roads leading to this popular tourist location. The Beachy Head service was still operated wholly by Southdown but following deregulation in 1986 would become joint with Eastbourne Buses. *Dave Brown*

Left: In 1980 Eastbourne Borough Council purchased from Ipswich Borough Transport four 1968 Leyland Atlanteans with Eastern Coach Works bodywork, and in 1985 two of these were smartly converted to open-top. The pair were later named and given individual liveries, as exemplified by 66 (LDX 76G) *Eastbourne King*, seen passing the Martello Tower (now known as the 'Wish Tower') *en route* to Beachy Head; 65 (LDX 75G) was named *Eastbourne Queen* and painted red and cream. The Western Lawns, shown here, was the site for both the 90th-anniversary and centenary celebrations for Eastbourne Buses, which is proud to be one of only 17 (at the time of writing) surviving municipally owned bus companies. *Dave Brown*

Below left: By the 1970s the standard Eastbourne Borough Council bus was the East Lancs-bodied Leyland Atlantean, which was to serve it well for many years. No 34 (YJK 934V) of the 1979 delivery features in this night-time view from February 1990, at which time a 'bus war' was raging between Eastbourne Buses and Hastings & District; behind is one of the latter's Mercedes minibuses. At this time it was still in vogue to rent televisions from Visionhire, and Wimpy was the place to go locally for 'fast food'. *John Bishop*

Right: Early in 1981, when deregulation was more than five years off, independent Vernon's Coaches of Westham, near Pevensey, identified the need for a service to/from the East Sussex village of Cowbeech. Seen in Terminus Road, one-time East Kent AEC Regent V/ Park Royal PFN 882 waits to depart with an obviously enthusiastic crew. *John Bishop*

Below right: Vernon's Coaches' Eastbourne–Cowbeech service saw good loads, as is demonstrated by this September 1986 view of passengers queuing to board ex-Lancaster City Council (via Maidstone Borough) Leyland Leopard/Pennine STD 121L in High Street, Hailsham. Soon Eastbourne Buses would provide the service, but eventually the route would cease, concluding this all-too-brief chapter. *John Bishop*

Above: Upon its acquisition in 1949 of Beacon Motor Services Southdown inherited the local town service in Crowborough and a depot in Western Road, Jarvis Brook, which became the company's most northeasterly outpost. In August 1963 its allocation included 632 (MUF 632), a 1954 Leyland Tiger Cub bodied by Duple subsidiary Nudd Bros & Lockyer, seen parked in London Road, close to Crowborough Cross. Perhaps the town's main claim to fame is that Sir Arthur Conan Doyle, creator of Sherlock Holmes, once captained the local golf club. *Dave Warren*

Right: Other than the loss of the bus station closing, Uckfield's High Street has changed very little since this photograph was taken in the late 1960s, although the vehicular content certainly has. Long gone are the East Lancs-bodied Leyland PD2s, typified by 807 (RUF 207), and the Marshall-bodied Leyland Leopards such as 687 (287 AUF), sold to East Kent in 1971. Note also the line-up of British-built motor cars and the once commonplace red telephone box. *Dave Brown*

A study of arguably the perfect British bus in Maidstone & District's distinctive livery of dark green and cream with silver roof, at Uckfield: all-Leyland PD2 DH387 (NKT 883) basks in the sunshine, awaiting departure for Brighton on route 122 in the late 1960s.

The letters 'DH' denoted a highbridge double-deck type. The bus looks almost bare without advertisements on the side and the even more familiar *Kent Messenger* posters on the front. *Malcolm Keeping*

Our next view at Uckfield features the rear of the bus station, where today Bell Lane links the town centre with the main A22 London–Eastbourne road. An Albion Nimbus bodied in Hove by Thos Harrington, Maidstone & District SO317 (317 LKK) of 1960 was photographed in the late 1960s. The bus had arrived on route 79 and, once loaded, would make the circuitous journey back to Tunbridge Wells via the East Sussex villages of Hadlow Down and Mayfield. *Malcolm Keeping*

Above: Seen in Uckfield in the autumn of 1968, Maidstone & District all-Leyland PD2/12 DH409 (NKT 905) heads south for Brighton on route 122, in direct competition with the railway. At this time Uckfield, on the main line between Brighton and Tunbridge Wells, still had a level crossing and a substantial station. The following year the line south of Uckfield would close, and nowadays Uckfield station, reduced to a single-platform affair on the other side of the road, serves as the terminus of the line from Oxted. *Dave Brown*

Right: It is summer 1975 in Uckfield, and the railway line south to Lewes has closed, but the station (in the background) remains in use, and the level crossing continues to be a hindrance to motorists! By now the NBC era is upon us, and for Southdown the vehicle policy involved the purchase of the Leyland Atlantean AN68, one of which, 725 (PUF 725M), is seen in the bus station. Possibly of more interest, however, is ex-Brighton, Hove & District Bristol Lodekka 2080 (JPM 80D) in the far distance. Both buses were on a Southdown Enthusiasts' Club tour. The bus station itself is no more, the site now being occupied by shops. *Malcolm Keeping*

Left: Forest Row, near East Grinstead, was the terminus of London Transport Country Area route 409. However, by September 1974 the route had passed to London Country Bus Services and was being operated *inter alia* by AEC/Park Royal Routemaster RCL2237 (CUV 237C), a one-time Green Line coach demoted to bus work. The vehicle is seen at the site of the old Forest Row railway station, closed in 1967 along with the East Grinstead–Tunbridge Wells West line. *John Bishop*

Above: Still employed on Green Line work, London Country Routemaster RCL2226 (CUV 226C) waits outside its owner's East Grinstead garage in October 1973 prior to taking up duty on route 709 to London. The 'GD' plate on the vehicle's nearside denotes allocation to Godstone garage; both this and East Grinstead were inherited from London Transport, but regrettably both have since closed. *John Bishop*

Left: London Country Daimler Fleetline/Park Royal XF8 (CUV 58C) close to the Surrey border in Lingfield Road, East Grinstead. The bus was one of eight such vehicles new to London Transport, having been purchased along with 50 Leyland Atlanteans to assess the suitability of the rear-engined layout and one-man operation. When this photograph was taken in the mid-1970s it was still in London Country's short-lived green and yellow, although the wheels had already succumbed to the standard NBC grey. *Malcolm Keeping*

Above: With the East Grinstead garage on the left and the bridge over the main railway line to London in the background, London Transport AEC Regal IV RF226 (MLL 763) is seen between journeys on route 436 to Imberhorne Estate in the early spring of 1966. Little could we have known that within four years London Transport's Country Area routes would come under the control of the National Bus Company, leading to the loss of such icons as the traditional 'bullseye' bus-stop flags. *John Bishop*

Left: On 1 July 1966 Crawley bus station was host to Southdown 1956 Guy Arab IV/ Park Royal 530 (PUF 630), seen between journeys on local route 76 to Gossops Green, one of the estates built as part of the rapid postwar development of this New Town. Nowadays it is difficult to imagine Southdown operating in Crawley, local services having been relinquished in the early 1970s as part of an NBC-inspired reorganisation. *Dave Warren*

Above: Crawley bus station on a bright, cold 6 February 1975, when one could still find buses in their original London Transport Country Area green, as worn by one-time Green Line Routemaster RCL2254 (albeit here relieved by London Country's canary-yellow waistband). Two AEC Swifts jockey for position behind, but taking pride of place is AN96 (MPJ 196L), a Leyland Atlantean/ Metro-Cammell dating from 1972 and one of many buses nationally to be adorned during the 1970s as an overall advertisement for London & Manchester Assurance. *John Bishop*

Left: Before the construction of the A264 by-pass all east–west traffic around Horsham had to pass through the town centre, including Crawley Road, where this view of London Country AEC Swift MB113 (VLW 113G) was recorded on 2 May 1970. The bus is still in London Transport Country Area green but with yellow (in lieu of cream) waistband, although the new company's 'flying polo' emblem has yet to be applied. The Metro-Cammell bodywork is enhanced by unpainted aluminium mouldings, which feature was retained when these vehicles first donned NBC leaf green. *Dave Warren*

Above: Southdown's garage at Horsham always seemed to have a well-kept appearance, with Virginia creeper over the front and the rear and, as seen in this view, beds planted with flowers. Marshall-bodied Bristol RESL 240 (KUF 240F) is seen when almost new in 1968. Note the destination screen displaying 'ON HIRE TO ALDERSHOT & DISTRICT TRACTION CO.LTD'. Within a few years Aldershot & District would merge with Thames Valley to become Alder Valley, as NBC rationalised its operations. *Malcolm Keeping*

Left: Haywards Heath was traditionally in East Sussex but following the unpopular local-government changes of 1974 found itself 'moved' into West Sussex. By the mid-1980s the NBC era was drawing to a close, as is apparent from this view of a pair of Southdown Leyland Nationals in Perrymount Road. The town's bus station, just out of shot to the left of this picture, had closed some years before, leaving vehicles to stop in the street. On the right is dual-door 78 (YCD 78T), in the recently revived apple green and cream but still bearing the NBC 'double-N' symbol, on the then recently introduced 781 route between Eastbourne and Gatwick; on the left, single-door 30 (PCD 76R) unusually wears all-over apple green, applied in haste to cover scorching sustained in a depot fire at Eastbourne in December 1985 and to which cream window surrounds were never added. *John Bishop*

Left: By the early 1990s Brighton Buses was expanding into more rural areas, as evidenced by this view of Leyland National 86 (OKJ 511M) in The Brow, Burgess Hill, in August 1991. This location has changed little, but the bus scene has, Brighton Buses having been consigned to the history books along with the Leyland National marque. This bus had a varied career: acquired by Southdown from Maidstone & District in 1980, it passed (following Deregulation in 1986) to Eastbourne Buses and thence to Brighton Buses. For the bus enthusiast the late 1980s and early '90s were interesting times indeed! *John Bishop*

The section of Station Road in Burgess Hill has changed little, including the station itself and the Railway Tavern. This view recorded on 18 June 1997 reflects the recent changes in the provision of public transport locally; services in Burgess Hill and Haywards Heath had latterly been operated by Brighton Blue Bus but following the takeover of that concern in May 1997 by Go-Ahead Group were operated by Brighton & Hove until relinquished upon re-tendering by West Sussex County Council in 2001. Pictured is Brighton & Hove 347 (F47 XPR), a Mercedes-Benz 811D with Wadham Stringer bodywork, one of 19 such vehicles acquired when nearly new in 1990 from Yellow Buses, Bournemouth; since sold for further service, some still visit Burgess Hill in the ownership of RDH Services, an independent operator based in Plumpton, East Sussex. *Gerald Mead*

Lewes is the County Town of East Sussex, but street scenes with transport interest are surprisingly difficult to come by. It is thus fortunate that one of the few to come to light should feature an operator which is no more, the Maidstone & District identity having been abandoned in recent years by Arriva. Back in 1993, Brighton-bound on route 729 from Tunbridge Wells, Northern Counties-bodied Leyland Olympian 5894 (F894 BKK) makes its way up the High Street; in the background is Cliffe High Street, which narrow thoroughfare once formed part of the main road through the town and was crossed by a bridge carrying the Tunbridge Wells–Brighton railway line. Recently renumbered 29, the bus service linking these towns is nowadays shared by Arriva and Brighton & Hove, the latter operator providing most journeys. *Dave Brown*

Having climbed the steep, lower section of Lewes High Street known as School Hill,
Southdown Bristol VR/ECW 283 (MGR 671P) turns into Market Street. Acquired in
1986 from Devon General, this bus continued to operate for some while in poppy red —
hitherto unthinkable for a Southdown vehicle. Note (right) the war memorial, focus for
the town's (in)famous Bonfire Night celebrations. *Malcolm Keeping*

Above: No book on rural Sussex would be complete without a view of Alfriston, nestling between the South Downs in the Cuckmere valley. In the late 1980s Brighton Buses (formerly Brighton Corporation) started a network of 'Countrybus' routes — basically circular trips, centred on Brighton, around the picturesque parts of the county. One such, the A2, covered East Sussex, including Alfriston, as seen in this view of 32 (LUF 132F) a 1968 Leyland PD3 with Metro-Cammell bodywork converted in 1979 to open-top. The traffic warden strutting along the High Street is no doubt clearing the way through the narrow thoroughfare. Regrettably the large tree on the left has now gone, opening up the square but robbing it of much of its former character. *Dave Brown*

Right: The River Cuckmere in East Sussex has its source north of Hailsham and before reaching the English Channel at Cuckmere Haven flows through a gap in the South Downs at Alfriston. Seen heading for Seaford, with the Downs providing a picturesque backdrop, is Brighton Buses 35 (MCD 135F), a 1968 Leyland PD3/4 with Metro-Cammell bodywork converted to open-top in 1979. This section of road, known as 'High & Over', is a gruelling test for many a vehicle and frequently results in a convoy of cars forming behind! *Dave Brown*

Above: For many years seafront route 17 was a flagship service for Brighton and Hove, allowing holidaymakers to see many of the attractions of both towns, from Rottingdean in the east to Portslade in the west. However, there remain areas where development has not encroached, notably the downland at Ovingdean, where this view was recorded of Southdown 2010 (RPN 10) on 11 April 1977. A Bristol Lodekka FS6B with ECW body, this bus was originally No 10 in the fleet of Brighton, Hove & District, finished in all-over cream with black bonnet, but still looks smart in NBC leaf green, thanks to the standard of finish achieved by staff at Portslade Works. *Dave Warren*

Right: Sussex is synonymous with the rolling South Downs with a windmill to take full advantage of the prevailing winds, as here at Rottingdean, near Brighton. The windmill is in the course of having its sweeps restored as Brighton & Hove Dennis Trident 820 (T820 RFG), with convertible-open-top East Lancs bodywork, speeds by *en route* for Brighton and Devil's Dyke on 14 July 2003. Although this is a recent view the company's livery has since changed to one featuring wavy lines and swirls. *Gerald Mead*

Above: The county's largest town (and now a city), Brighton has long been a popular destination for coaches, on both express and excursion work. In the early 1970s MJG 44, a 1957 Beadle-bodied AEC Reliance of East Kent, in that company's deep red and cream, nears journey's end in the Old Steine. On the right an unidentified Leyland Titan of Brighton Corporation waits on the 41/42 stand at the bottom of St James's Street, just as the trolleybuses had years before. This part of Brighton has changed very little in the intervening years, but alas the richly coloured coaches of yesteryear are now but a memory. *Dave Brown*

Above right: In years gone by enthusiasts in the Brighton area would go to the town's Whitehawk Road coach park to see coaches from far and wide. Imagine, then, their dismay when the adjoining council estate was redeveloped and expanded, leading to the loss of this haven! Among the visitors on 19 June 1966, by which time building work was well underway, was 106 AUL, a Plaxton-bodied Ford Thames 570E belonging to Warren's Coaches of Ticehurst, near Wadhurst, East Sussex. *Dave Warren*

Right: Years ago a trip up Edward Street in Brighton would reveal either building sites or derelict buildings — but they made great places for visiting coaches to park! Seen here in June 1968 is Bedford VAM/Duple EHC 800F, belonging to Jackson's of Eastbourne. Visible in the background are (left) the new John Street Police Station and (right) the old St John's School, still avoiding demolition. This site in the foreground has since been redeveloped and is now occupied by the imposing American Express building. *Dave Warren*

Left: **Streets of Sussex** would not be complete without a look at Regency Brighton, here serving as a backdrop to Brighton & Hove Scania N113/East Lancs 780 (R880 HCD) of 1998. Seen on 23 September 1998 in 'black stripe' livery (now fast disappearing), the bus is heading along Marine Parade, bound for Newhaven on route 14, which forms part of an intensive service covering the whole of the A259 coast road between Brighton and Eastbourne. *Gerald Mead*

Above: In May 1969, when this photograph was taken, Brush-bodied Leyland TD1 0813 (UF 4813) of 1929 was the pride of Southdown Motor Services, having been retained by the company as a preserved vehicle. Fitted with a petrol engine (which she retains today), she was a very smooth if expensive runner. Looking absolutely immaculate, she was participating in the annual London–Brighton Historic Commercial run, being seen on Brighton seafront. The garage on the left was owned by Hannington's — 'Brighton's Leading Department Store' — but despite an extensive refit has since made way for flats. The line-up of British motorcycles would today gladden the heart of many an enthusiast. *Dave Brown*

Left: Brighton Corporation AEC Regent III/Weymann 81 (HUF 81), dating from 1947, in Brighton's Old Steine, at the junction with St James's Street. In the 1960s Corporation vehicles were all still red and cream, but the fleet would soon adopt the new livery of blue and white. Routes 26A and 46A (displayed on the following PD2) inter-worked to form a circular route — a practice carried over from tram and trolleybus days. *Dave Brown*

Above: Resplendent in its smart livery of red and cream finished off by the town crest, Brighton Corporation 91 (KCD 91), a Weymann-bodied AEC Regent III dating from 1950, speeds down Queen's Park Road on 11 October 1964. This part of Brighton has changed little since the days when the area was developed other than by the encroachment of the internal-combustion engine, and the complete lack of cars in this view is noteworthy. Note also the lamp standards, which five years previously had supported the trolleybus overhead. *Dave Warren*

Above: A Leyland PD3/4 with Metro-Cammell body, Brighton Corporation 32 (LUF 132F) speeds along Brighton's Lewes Road, heading towards the town centre, in September 1977. Inclusion of this picture makes for an interesting comparison with that of the same bus in later open-top form in Alfriston (see page 38). Such an uncluttered scene would be near-impossible to capture today, as the city struggles to cope with ever-increasing numbers of cars. *Dave Brown*

Right: Elm Grove, Brighton, connecting the Lewes Road (seen at the bottom of the hill) and the racecourse, used to be served by trams and later (from 1939) by trolleybuses until the Elm Grove routes were converted to motor bus in 1959. One of the trolleybus routes, serving the Queen's Park area, was the 42, upon which Brighton Corporation Leyland Atlantean/Willowbrook 85 (TUF 85J) of 1971 is seen tackling the steep climb in May 1982. *John Bishop*

Left: Brighton's Race Hill has long been a terminus for local public transport, notably tram route E, trolleybus route 43A and motor-bus route 2, while on race days the racecourse itself was a popular destination for private hires. So employed on a sunny 7 August 1969 was a brand-new Southdown dual-purpose Leyland Leopard/Northern Counties, 456 (NUF 456G), looking absolutely immaculate in the unusual (and short-lived) two-tone green applied to these vehicles. *Dave Warren*

Above: Enthusiasts of a certain age will always remember Southdown's head office as being at 5 Steine Street, Brighton, (by the coach station) rather than Southdown House, the concrete-and-glass block erected in later years next to Freshfield Road garage. However, it is the latter building which features in this view of 1971 Leyland Leopard/Plaxton 1828 (UUF 328J), recorded on 29 June 1980. In the days of white coaches the painting of a number of this batch to celebrate Southdown's 65th anniversary provided welcome relief from a sea of leaf green. In 2005 Southdown Motor Services is celebrating 90 years; where, we ask, did the last 25 years go? *Dave Warren*

Above: In the mid-1960s Government policy freed Bristol Commercial Vehicles and Eastern Coach Works to supply vehicles to operators then outside State control, including Southdown. Having already purchased a number of Marshall-bodied Bristol RE saloons, in 1971 the company (by now part of NBC) took delivery of a trio of RELL models with ECW bodywork, and how attractive these looked in green and cream with traditional scroll fleetname. Pictured when new in Brighton's London Road is 602 (UCD 602J). Behind the trees and the typical Brighton-style concrete bus shelter is St Peter's Church, Parish Church of Brighton since 1873 but sadly today under threat of closure, on account of the cost of much-needed roof repairs. *Malcolm Keeping*

Right: Off the main Lewes Road in Brighton are a number of estates, including Bevendean. Passing the small parade of shops in Lower Bevendean Avenue in the early 1970s is Eastern Coach Works-bodied Daimler Fleetline 391 (XUF 391K) on route 110, which was always a preserve of Southdown. However, Daimler chassis came into the fleet only in NBC days, while the small, modernised fleetname was a shortlived style which would soon give way to NBC corporate identity. Note also the once familiar cream bonnet of the black Streamline taxi following. *Malcolm Keeping*

Left: When this scene was recorded in June 1971 the visitor (or resident) travelling to Brighton's Old Steine via the London Road would pass along this avenue of trees and gardens. Now the trees have gone, victims of the great storm of October 1987, and one encounters bus lanes and traffic lights. With this in mind, savour this view of Brighton Corporation Leyland PD2/ Weymann Aurora 11 (5011 CD), one of a batch of 16 purchased in 1961 to permit the second stage of trolleybus replacement and still working a former trolleybus route some 10 years later. Within a short time the bus would forsake its attractive red and cream for the Corporation's then new livery of French blue and white. *Dave Brown*

Above: Overlooked by many a photographer is the rear aspect — the proverbial 'back end of a bus'! This view, recorded at Brighton's Old Steine in June 1971, features Brighton Corporation 33 (LUF 133F), a Leyland PD3/4 with Metro-Cammell Orion body. Note the advertisement for John Beal & Sons' bookshop in nearby East Street, which premises are still used today by Sussex Stationers. *Dave Brown*

Above: Devil's Dyke, north of Brighton and Hove, on 1 September 1963, when one could breeze up to this beauty spot, some 750ft above sea level, in a rebuilt wartime Southdown Guy Arab. This view depicts 444 (GUF 144), rebuilt in 1950, and 439 (GUF 139), rebuilt with upper-deck windscreen in 1959 and here on a Southdown Enthusiasts' Club tour. Soon the mellifluous whine of the Gardner 5LW engine would be heard no more, replaced by the gurgle of the Leyland O.600. *Dave Warren*

Right: Old and (relatively) new Southdown open-toppers at Brighton's Palace Pier in the summer of 1970, in the form of 1929 Brush-bodied Leyland TD1 013 (UF 4813) and 1964 Leyland PD3/Northern Counties 411 (411 DCD). The former was operating a 'vintage' service to Rottingdean, whilst 411 was preparing to depart on the lengthy 102 route to Arundel, in West Sussex. Adding to the holiday atmosphere is a line of deck chairs, albeit with no takers. *Dave Brown*

Above: Brighton's Pool Valley bus station was the terminus for country routes, provided in the main by Southdown but also by Maidstone & District. In the mid-1960s Leylands predominated, just one Guy — a Southdown Arab IV/Park Royal — being visible here. Apparently standing aloof, with blinds set for route 18 to Hawkhurst in Kent, is Maidstone & District all-Leyland PD2/12 DH394 (NKT 890), complete with *Kent Messenger* advertisements on either side of the destination display. *Malcolm Keeping*

Right: A slightly later view of Pool Valley, with two Southdown Leyland Titans waiting to depart for destinations in West Sussex. Northern Counties-bodied PD3/4 'Queen Mary' 251 (BUF 251C) of 1965 (left) will head along the coast to Littlehampton, while Beadle-bodied PD2/12 782 (RUF 182) dating from 1956 — and, it must be said, somewhat in need of a clean — will take the picturesque route 22 inland to Petworth. *Dave Brown*

Left: Our final look at Pool Valley dates from 1987. We are now in the deregulated era, and the NBC 'double N' logo has given way to Southdown's new symbol, which soon became known unofficially as 'Hissing Sid'! However, the biggest shock of all was the appearance of *red* Southdown buses, such as 624 (UTO 834S), a Bristol VR acquired in 1986 from Devon General and pressed into service without being repainted; confusingly, it also still displays its former operator's fleet number (618) as it waits to head west on coastal route 700 to Portsmouth. The buildings behind are some of the oldest surviving in this part of Brighton (or, as it was formerly known, 'Brighthelmstone') and feature in early prints depicting extensive flooding of the area *c*1850. *Malcolm Keeping*

Above: Brighton's Churchill Square shopping complex as first built had a very bland character, and when one actually views the building one can understand why it was rebuilt in current form. This mid-1980s view features Southdown East & Mid Sussex Bristol VR/ECW 620 (UWV 620S). The bus has a detachable roof for open-top services but is seen here in closed-top form on limited-stop service 729 to Tunbridge Wells. *Malcolm Keeping*

Above: Western Road, Brighton as we used to know it, with two-way traffic, the freedom to park where and when you liked and stores which could be identified from a distance by their fascias, such as British Home Stores and F. W. Woolworth. Add to this Brighton, Hove & District buses with comprehensive destination displays (so you knew exactly where they were going), and you have a nostalgic picture of the 1950s and '60s. Bound for Black Rock on route 4, the leading bus, Bristol K/ECW 387 (DNJ 996) of 1948, was one of a number fitted with a Bristol AVW engine; such buses emitted a very distinctive note and were noticeably more lively than their Gardner-engined counterparts. *Howard Butler*

Right: Seen passing through Brighton's Castle Square in June 1971, Southdown Bristol Lodekka FS6B/ECW 2019 (RPN 19) makes for Whitehawk, in East Brighton. New in 1960 as Brighton, Hove & District 19, it is still in full red and cream livery, which was retained for a couple of years after Southdown's takeover of BH&D in 1969. Note the smart Rover P6 parked in Palace Place; also the despised parking meter, introduced as a source of revenue for traffic schemes! *Dave Brown*

Left: With brilliant sunshine highlighting the red-and-cream colours to create the ultimate in bus photography, Brighton, Hove & District 475 (JAP 513), a Bristol KSW6G/ECW of 1954, nears journey's end at Mackie Avenue, Patcham, on route 5B in the mid-1960s. The houses and roads retain a distinct 1930s feel, while the South Downs behind are as yet unscarred by the Brighton By-pass. *Howard Butler*

Above: Hove backs onto the South Downs, and some of the steeper roads in its Hangleton estate used to put Brighton, Hove & District's ECW-bodied Bristol KSW6G and KSW6B buses through their paces. One of the latter, with Bristol AVW engine, 431 (GNJ 996) turns into Amberley Drive, a short distance from the terminus of route 11 at the popular Grenadier Hotel, on 25 June 1966. *Dave Warren*

Left: In the late 1960s, with passenger numbers diminishing, Brighton Corporation judged that Dyke Road route 52 did not require double-deckers and so ordered a batch of Leyland Panther Cub single-deckers, with either Strachans or Marshall bodywork. Depicted is one of the three Strachans-bodied examples, 38 (NUF 138G), seen heading down Queen's Road towards the Clock Tower on 11 May 1969. The area of Brighton near the railway station has since been 'improved' by numerous traffic-management schemes, but at this time traffic still travelled either way, unhindered by bus lanes and traffic lights. Readers are assured that the removal business (right) was not a secret sideline of the author's! *Dave Warren*

Above: Upon the demise of the trams in 1939 Brighton Corporation introduced Dyke Road routes 51 and 52, worked initially by AEC Regent double-deckers, which ran to the original tram terminus at Tivoli Crescent; later the 52 was extended to venture into pastures new for Brighton Corporation, in the Borough of Hove — unheard of in previous years. The new terminus was in Queen Victoria Avenue, Goldstone Valley, where Marshall-bodied Leyland Panther Cub 39 (NUF 139G), freshly repainted from red and cream to blue and white, is seen on 6 July 1970. Note how Brighton Corporation made maximum use of advertising space on its vehicles. *Dave Warren*

Left: For the 1971 season Southdown again used 1929 Leyland TD1 open-topper 0813 (UF 4813) on a 'vintage' service, this time on flatter terrain, between Brighton's Palace Pier and Hove's King Alfred swimming baths, opposite which it is seen here. The buildings in the background survive today, carefully maintained as part of Hove's heritage, while the bus, still owned by Southdown, is in the care of Amberley Chalk Pits Museum. *Dave Warren*

Above: With its wide roads and spacious promenades, Hove has always had a quieter and more sedate feel than bustling Brighton, as is apparent from this mid-1960s view of Brighton, Hove & District Bristol K5G/ECW 991 (GHT 126), purchased from Bristol Tramways and rebuilt by the company as an open-topper and seen here in the company of such classic British cars as the Ford Zephyr (parked), Humber Hawk, Hillman Minx and the Ford 105E Anglia. In the distance (right), beyond a Southdown Leyland Tiger Cub/Beadle coach, can be seen the King Alfred swimming baths — once the envy of many a town but today under imminent threat of demolition — while on the left is Hove College for Boys, which has long since closed its doors. *Howard Butler*

Left: The main shopping thoroughfare in Hove is Church Road. Approaching the Town Hall on route 49A in May 1973, Brighton Corporation Leyland PD2/ Weymann 53 (WCD 53) trundles along an almost deserted road, followed at a respectful distance by two Southdown Bristol FLF Lodekkas in all-over leaf green. Alas the PD2 would be withdrawn and sold within three months. *John Bishop*

Above: At the western end of Portland Road, Hove, is Portslade railway station, built in the distinctive architectural style of the erstwhile London, Brighton & South Coast Railway and seen behind Brighton Buses East Lancs-bodied Dennis Dominator 43 (JSL 284X) in April 1990. The bus had an interesting history, being one of five new to Tayside (Dundee) in 1981 and acquired by Brighton in 1985; after sale by Brighton Buses one was acquired by Eastbourne Buses, while three of the others (including this bus) headed north to join Chester City Transport. *John Bishop*

Above: Southdown 935 (6935 CD), one of the company's ubiquitous 'Queen Mary' Northern Counties-bodied Leyland PD3s, sets off for Lancing from Worthing seafront on 26 March 1971. Many of the buildings behind have since passed into history, although the distinctive roofline of the Dome Cinema remains a local landmark. The bus-stop flag is typical of those in the Worthing area, which featured red lettering on a white base in lieu of the more usual black on white. *Alan Snatt*

Right: Although by the time this photograph was taken— on 26 March 1971 — Southdown was part of the National Bus Company, outward appearances had changed little, and the familiar green and cream long associated with Sussex, with 'SOUTHDOWN' proudly emblazoned on the sides, still stood for comfort and reliability. No 374 (TCD 374J) a Northern Counties bodied Daimler Fleetline new the previous year, makes its way westwards along Worthing seafront, in a scene little changed today. *Alan Snatt*

Above: A Leyland Leopard with standard BET-style Marshall bodywork, 114 (114 CUF) is seen at Ringmer Road, Worthing, when virtually new on 8 February 1964. The black-on-white destination display looks odd and would be replaced by the normal white-on-black as soon as circumstance allowed. What, one wonders, had attracted the attention of the crew, staring into the front garden of the house on the right? *Dave Warren*

Right: New in 1969/70 and allocated to the (red) Brighton, Hove & District fleet, Southdown's first batch of 10 Daimler Fleetlines — 33ft long, with dual-door Northern Counties bodywork — were followed later in 1970 by 15 single-door, 30ft buses delivered in green and cream. With their curved windscreens they looked very stylish, as demonstrated by 382 (TCD 382J) in the early 1970s near Worthing Central station. On the left is the main garage of H. D. Steele & Son; a replica of an early garage belonging to this firm is to be found at the Chalk Pits Museum at Amberley, West Sussex. *Malcolm Keeping*

Above: The answer for holidaymakers when it was wet was to go on an excursion, and how better than by Harrington-bodied Leyland Royal Tiger, as here on Worthing seafront. In 1963 local firm Buck's Coaches had been taken over by Southdown, which company retained the former's name and livery for two years. Car 1832 (OUF 832) would thus continue to wear these attractive colours for only a short time when photographed on 7 November 1965. *Dave Warren*

Right: With its splendid castle Arundel, seat of the Duke and Duchess of Norfolk, has always been a magnet for visitors, many of whom in days gone by would have arrived by Southdown bus from Brighton. This charming scene dating from the summer of 1968 depicts Park Royal-bodied Leyland PD2/12 No 768 (OCD 768) commencing its return journey on route 10. The castle entrance is just visible at the top of the hill in the background. *Dave Brown*

Left: In Petworth, West Sussex, walls and buildings blend to form an attractive town which has changed little over the years, although the narrow streets are less than accommodating to an 8ft-wide bus! In this late-1960s scene Southdown Leyland PD2/East Lancs 798 (RUF 198) pauses before returning to Horsham as a dray delivers its valuable cargo. *Dave Brown*

Above: For the traveller heading west, Midhurst is the last town in West Sussex before reaching Hampshire. Seen in March 1968, all-Leyland PD2/12 754 (MCD 754) — numerically the last of its type delivered to the company, in 1953 — pauses in North Street *en route* for Bognor Regis. As well as being a source of travel information, the Southdown booking/enquiries office (right) would have doubled as a parcels office in the days when the company provided a delivery service. *Dave Brown*

Left: In days gone by a visit to the Southdown garage behind the splendid art-deco bus station in Bognor Regis, West Sussex, would reveal many interesting vehicles parked during the day in the open, but in more recent times the opportunity has been lost, with the closure in the early 1980s of both garage and bus station. Taking pride of place on 14 October 1968 was recently delivered 228 (KUF 228F), a Marshall-bodied Bristol RESL, while lining the perimeter of the yard were a selection of Leyland Leopard buses and coaches as well as another Bristol RESL and a Leyland Tiger Cub. *Alan Snatt*

Below left: One location that has changed little today is Chichester bus station, nowadays the Head Office of Southdown Motor Services. Present on 14 October 1968, with the (then) almost-new Crown Court as a backdrop, were two of the company's fine 'Queen Mary' Leyland PD3 double-deckers. Taking centre stage is 287 (FCD 287D) of 1966, while on the right is an earlier example fitted with an illuminated advertisement panel but lacking the refinement of twin headlights. The wall behind, employing local flint, is built to traditional style and typical of many that once lined the streets of Sussex. *Alan Snatt*

Back cover: It is hard to believe that Ovingdean in Brighton can appear so rural when within minutes one can be amidst the hustle and bustle of modern-day life. This view features the last Southdown bus still in BH&D red and cream, Bristol RESL/ECW 2206 (PPM 206G), on a Southdown Enthusiasts' Club tour on 18 January 1975. Note that, despite the winter sunshine, there is still snow on the edge of the road.
John Bishop